GUPPIES in TUXEDOS

MARVIN TERBAN

GUPPIES in TUXEDOS

Funny Eponyms

illustrated by
GIULIO MAESTRO

CLARION BOOKS
NEW YORK

Thanks to the United States Trademark Association for supplying the following information: Buick, Cadillac, Chevrolet, Oldsmobile, and Pontiac are registered trademarks of General Motors Corporation. Ford, Mercury, and Lincoln are registered trademarks of Ford Motor Company. Chrysler, Plymouth, and Dodge are registered trademarks of the Chrysler Corporation. Levi's is a registered trademark of Levi Strauss & Co. Jacuzzi is a registered trademark of Jacuzzi Inc. Frisbee is a registered trademark of Kransco. Listerine is a registered trademark of Warner-Lambert Company.

Clarion Books
a Houghton Mifflin Company imprint
215 Park Avenue South, New York, NY 10003
Text copyright © 1988 by Marvin Terban
Illustrations copyright © 1988 by Giulio Maestro
First Clarion paperback edition, 1988; reissued, 2008.

www.clarionbooks.com

Printed in the U.S.A.

The Library of Congress has cataloged the original edition as follows:
Terban, Marvin.
Guppies in tuxedos: funny eponyms / by Marvin Terban ;
illustrated by Giulio Maestro.
p. cm.
Bibliography: p.
Summary: Traces the origins of more than 100 eponymous words—
words derived from the names of people or places.
ISBN 0-89919-509-1
1. English language—Eponyms—Juvenile literature.
2. English language—Etymology—Juvenile literature.
[1. English language— Eponyms. 2. English language—Etymology]
I. Maestro, Giulio, ill.   II. Title.
PE1596.T48   1988
422—dc19

PA ISBN: 978-0-547-03188-0

EW   10 9 8 7 6 5 4 3 2 1

To Karen
If you were an eponym,
"karen" would mean "a wonderful wife."

Contents

Introduction

Where do words come from? There are hundreds of thousands of words in English. Some words come from people's names. If a person does something very important, or beneficial, or even terrible, his or her name can actually become a word.

A person whose name becomes a word is called an eponym (pronounced EP-uh-nim). Years go by and we forget about the person but keep using the eponymous (pronounced eh-PON-uh-mus) words. (Eponymous words are what we call the words that come from eponyms.)

This book will introduce you to the people behind over 100 eponymous words, who they were and why they became eponyms. Sometimes the names of places become words, and many of them are in this book too.

Maybe one day you'll do something so interesting, so wonderful, so extraordinary that your name will become a word in the English language. You'll be an eponym!

° 1 °

Food

Did you know that you eat eponymous foods all the time? The names of many common dishes—and some fancy ones, too—come from the names of people or places. Here's a tasty assortment of them. You might find some in your lunch box. Let's start with three everyday foods named after the places they came from.

Bologna

Bologna, a picturesque city of northern Italy, was famous for its seasoned smoked sausages made of mixed meats. When people all over the world started eating the sausage from Bologna, they called it "bologna" and sometimes spelled it "baloney."

Frankfurter and Hamburger

Frankfurters, nicknamed "hot dogs," are sold at every professional baseball game in America, but they came from **Frankfurt** in Germany. Millions of grilled hamburgers on toasted buns with pickles and ketchup are eaten every day in America, but these meat patties were first cooked up in **Hamburg**, Germany.

Cheeses

LIMBURGER is a soft, white cheese with a very strong odor. Some people hold their noses near this cheese. It's named after the place where it was first made, a province in Belgium called **Limburg**.

ROQUEFORT is a strong, cream-colored cheese with a blue mold running through it. It originated in the French town of **Roquefort**.

CHEDDAR is a hard, smooth cheese. It can be white or yellow, mild or sharp. The first time anybody ever ate cheddar cheese was in a village in England named **Cheddar**.

Pickles

Before refrigerators were invented, foods were "pickled"—preserved in salt water or vinegar. In the 1300s a Dutchman, **Willem Beukelz** (pronounced BOY-kells), was the first person to "pickle" food. English people liked Beukelz's idea, but they mispronounced "Beukelz" so that it sounded like "pickles." Today we call pickled cucumbers "pickles."

Sandwich

The British **Earl of Sandwich** loved to gamble. Sometimes he stayed at the card table for a whole day and night. He didn't want to get up to eat or get his fingers messy, so early one card-playing morning in 1762, he ordered his servant to bring him roast beef wrapped in bread. The idea caught on!

Graham Cracker

Reverend **Sylvester Graham** hated meat, alcohol, and white bread. He wrote books and lectured people in the 1800s to give up such "unnatural" foods and drink. He invented his own healthful cracker baked of unsifted whole wheat flour. Some people thought Graham was crazy, but his crackers are still popular.

Candy

In the 1600s, little French **Prince Charles de Condé** (pronounced con-DAY) loved sugary treats. The royal chef was worried that the boy wasn't eating healthful foods, so he glazed bits of meat, vegetables, and fruit with sugar, egg whites, and nuts. Today just the coatings of Prince de Condé's sweet treats are called "candy."

Pasteurized Milk

"Milk" doesn't come from an eponym, but "pasteurized" does. **Louis Pasteur**, a French scientist in the 1800s, developed a way to destroy harmful germs in foods and beverages. He heated them to a high temperature, then chilled them quickly. The bacteria were killed and the food stayed fresh longer! Naturally, this process is named after its inventor.

Here are some foods you probably won't find in your lunch box:

Charlotte Russe

A royal chef once made a crown of ladyfingers (finger-shaped sponge cakes) and filled it with jellied custard. He named the fancy pastry "charlotte russe" in honor of **Princess Charlotte**, the only daughter of King George IV of England in the 1800s. The king loved it. So did Charlotte. So does almost everyone who's eaten one since.

Melba Toast and Peach Melba

Nellie Melba (1861 – 1931), a famous and plump Australian opera singer, was always on a diet. At a fancy London hotel, she ordered her breakfast toast extra-thin to cut a few calories. By mistake it came out extra-burnt, but it tasted so delicious that the hotel put the toast on the menu and named it in honor of Miss Melba. Later, the opera star wanted a special new dessert for a party. A famous French chef poured raspberry sauce over peaches and ice cream and called the concoction "peach melba." What happened to Nellie's diet?

Beef Stroganoff and Beef Wellington

These two fancy beef dinners were named after famous figures in nineteenth-century history: **Count Paul Stroganoff**, a Russian diplomat, and the **Duke of Wellington**, a military hero and British prime minister.

Napoleon

Have you ever eaten a delicious, flaky, custard cream pastry called a "napoleon"? Many people think that it's named after Napoleon, the emperor of France in the early 1800s, who supposedly ate them in battle. That's not so. They were first made by Neapolitans, the people of Naples, Italy. The Neapolitans called the pastry "**Napolitain**." If you mispronounce "Napolitain" it sounds like "napoleon," and that's what happened!

Yum!

∘ 2 ∘

Clothes

Open your closet. Look in. See all those eponymous garments hanging there? Here are five familiar words that come from the names of people and three that come from the names of places.

Leotards

Jules Léotard was an amazing young French circus performer of the mid-nineteenth century. He thrilled Parisians with the world's first aerial somersault from a flying trapeze. He also designed his own costume: a stretchy, one-piece, body-hugging suit so he could fly through the air with the greatest of ease. He called it "natural garb," and today acrobats, dancers, and gymnasts wear "leotards."

Bloomers in bloomers!

Bloomers

Amelia Jenks Bloomer, editor of a nineteenth-century ladies' magazine, fought for women's rights. The long hoopskirts of that time were difficult to wear and picked up dirt. So in 1851 Bloomer put on a new two-piece sports outfit—baggy trousers gathered at the ankles worn under a short skirt. She shocked some people, but "bloomers" were popular for fifty years. Now the word refers jokingly to ladies' undergarments.

Cardigan

James Brudenell, **Lord Cardigan**, was a foolish, snobby, strict British general. He led his Light Brigade on a disastrous charge against the Russians in 1854. Most of his men were killed. But Lord Cardigan lived and became famous. So did the open, woolen sweater he wore to keep warm. Even today we call a collarless sweater with buttons and a round or V-neck a "cardigan."

Levi's®

Here's an eponymous word from a person's first name. In the mid-1800s thousands of people rushed to California to mine for gold. During this "gold rush," **Levi Strauss**, a German immigrant, manufactured heavy blue overalls with copper rivets to strengthen the pockets. Miners, who stuffed their pockets with chunks of ore, liked these trousers. Levi's® pants became popular, and today many people still wear them.

Pants

A famous funny character in many old Italian comedies of the fifteenth century was called **Pantaloon**. He was a skinny, silly, greedy, suspicious old man who always wore the same costume—slippers, a tight red vest, and red trousers. Soon all trousers were called "pantaloons" and then just "pants."

Jeans

"Jean" was originally the name of a strong, twilled cotton cloth. Today this cloth is used to make sportswear, work clothes, or trousers. The cloth was named after **Genoa**, the Italian city where it was first woven many years ago. In middle English, Genoa was spelled "Gene" or "Jean."

Tuxedo

In the late 1800s **Tuxedo Park** was a wealthy, exclusive New York community. One year, people were surprised when a rich man wore a new-style dark, formal suit with satin lapels and trouser stripes (instead of the traditional long tailcoat) to the Autumn Ball at the Tuxedo Park Country Club. Soon men all over the country were wearing these Tuxedo Park suits and calling them "tuxedos."

Bikini

In July 1946 the United States began testing atom bombs on a little island in the Pacific Ocean called **Bikini Atoll**. That same summer a very skimpy two-piece bathing suit was first modeled at a Paris fashion show. Some shocked people said that the daring swimsuits "hit the audience like an atom bomb," so they were called "bikinis."

∘ 3 ∘

Transportation

The world rides in and on vehicles—giant airships, plush railroad cars, popular automobiles, even a powerful engine—whose names are derived from eponyms.

Zeppelin

Ferdinand von Zeppelin, a German count, served in the American Civil War on the Union hot-air balloon staff. After he went back to Germany, many thought he was crazy trying to build a rigid "lighter-than-air" ship. But his huge "zeppelins" flew at about fifty miles an hour and dropped bombs on England, France, and Belgium during World War I. Thousands of people flew in "zeppelins," but after terrible accidents, the ships were no longer used.

Pull, man, pull!

Pullman Car

George Pullman invested all the money he earned digging for gold to build one luxurious railroad car for sitting and sleeping. But the car was too high and too wide for existing railroads. Two years later, in 1865, when the state of Illinois needed a fancy carriage for President Lincoln's funeral train, it widened stations, raised bridges, and rented Pullman's car. People loved it, railroads ordered the cars, and Pullman became a millionaire.

Diesel Engine

Rudolf Diesel, a German mechanical engineer, invented this heavy-duty internal-combustion engine in the late 1800s to replace the slow steam engine. Today heavy-power industrial equipment, big ships, locomotives, generators, trucks, submarines, and some cars are powered by "diesel" engines.

American Cars

All the popular American-made cars are named after eponyms—every one of them!

FORD®: Henry Ford was the chief engineer at the Edison Illuminating Company in Detroit before he organized the Ford Motor Company in 1903. Besides Ford cars, the Ford Motor Company makes two other automobiles:

MERCURY® is named after the mythological Roman god **Mercury**. In different stories he's the messenger of the gods, or the god of commerce, travel, skill with hands and body, eloquence, and thievery!

LINCOLN® is named in honor of the sixteenth president of the United States, **Abraham Lincoln** (1809–65). Lincoln was born too early to ever ride in a car.

CHRYSLER®: The Chrysler Corporation is named for **Walter P. Chrysler**, a one-time railroad engineer who was working for General Motors in 1924 when he started his own company. Besides Chrysler cars, the company makes two other automobiles:

PLYMOUTH® is named for **Plymouth, Massachusetts**, where the Pilgrims landed in 1620. A model of the Pilgrims' ship, *the Mayflower*, was the hood ornament on the first Plymouth cars.

DODGE®: Two brothers, **Horace and John Dodge**, became rich making engines for the Ford Motor Company. In about 1915, they manufactured the first Dodge Brothers car. Later, Dodge cars became part of the Chrysler company.

General Motors manufactures five eponymous autos:

BUICK®: David D. Buick was a successful plumbing inventor, but he liked cars better than pipes, so he started the Buick Manufacturing Company in 1903. Later it was taken over by General Motors.

CHEVROLET®: Louis Chevrolet was born in Switzerland and had been a Buick race-car driver. He founded the Chevrolet Motor Company in 1911, and a few years later the company became part of General Motors.

PONTIAC® was named after the Indian chief **Pontiac**, who died in 1769. Although Pontiac had led a famous attack on the British soldiers in Detroit, he later became their friend.

OLDSMOBILE®: Ransom E. Olds, an automobile inventor and builder, founded the Olds Motor Works in 1899. In 1901, the company began making the Oldsmobile car, the first commercially successful car in America.

CADILLAC® is the oldest car manufactured in Detroit. Its name honors **Antoine de la Mothe Cadillac**, a French explorer and army officer in America who founded the city of Detroit in 1701.

°4°

The United States

So many American states are named after people, you could almost say that America is an eponymous country. Here are some examples, beginning with "America" itself.

America

Who discovered America? Columbus? The Vikings? It was not **Amerigo Vespucci**, but that's who the country is named after. Why? Amerigo, an Italian, worked for a company that outfitted ships for Columbus and other navigators. He wrote stories about his own voyages around 1500, and many people believed that he had explored what is now North and South America. A young mapmaker was so impressed by Amerigo Vespucci's tales that he published a map of the New World and called it "America" to honor Amerigo. Later people thought Vespucci had only heard stories from sailors and pretended that he had made the voyages himself. Spain didn't believe him at all and called the new lands "Columbia" until the eighteenth century. By then so many other countries were calling our land "America" that Spain finally began calling it that too.

CALIFORNIA: Spanish settlers named this area after **Calafia**, the queen of an imaginary island in a sixteenth-century Spanish book. The island was supposed to be a paradise.

DELAWARE honors the first governor of Virginia colony, **Lord De La Warr**.

GEORGIA is named for **King George II** of England.

LOUISIANA honors **King Louis XIV** of France.

MARYLAND is named for **Queen Henrietta Maria**, wife of Charles I of England. It was first spelled "Marieland."

NEW MEXICO: "Mexico" commemorates the Aztec Indian war god **Mexitil**. Spanish explorers from Mexico named the American state Nuevo (New) Mexico.

NEW YORK was originally part of New Amsterdam. It was seized by the British from the Dutch and renamed for the British commander, the **Duke of York**.

NORTH CAROLINA and **SOUTH CAROLINA:** This area was named in honor of **King Charles I** of England and was first called "Carolana," from Carolus, the Latin word for "Charles." In 1710 the area was divided into North and South Carolina.

PENNSYLVANIA: King Charles II of England named this land. "Penn" honors **Sir William Penn**, father of the founder of the colony. *Sylvania* is the Latin word for "woods." So "Pennsylvania" means "Penn's Woods."

VIRGINIA and WEST VIRGINIA: Virginia was originally just one state. Sir Walter Raleigh named the area for **Queen Elizabeth I of England, the "Virgin Queen."** West Virginia split off in 1863.

WASHINGTON honors **George Washington**, the first president of the United States.

Places, too, can be eponymous. Here are two famous examples:

WASHINGTON, D.C., is named after **George Washington**, of course. "D.C." stands for "District of Columbia." "Columbia" honors **Christopher Columbus**. So do many other places in America—Columbus, Ohio; Columbia University, and many streets and schools named Columbus or Columbia.

THE BRONX: Years ago this borough of New York City was covered with farms, market villages, and country estates. **Jonas Bronck** built a large farm there in about 1640. He invited many friends to visit. They would say, "We're going to the Broncks' farm." Soon they just said, "We're going to the Broncks'." Later the spelling changed to "The Bronx."

Days and Months

The calendar is loaded with eponymous words. Here is a chance to meet the people who lent their names to the days and months.

Days

Five days of the week are named after people. Not real people, but very special people—ancient mythological gods and a goddess. Four of them are from one family.

TUESDAY is named for the ancient Scandinavian god of war **Tyr** (sometimes spelled **Tiw**). Tuesday was originally "Tyr's day" (or "Tiw's day.")

WEDNESDAY was originally "Woden's day." **Woden** was Tyr's father and the ruler of the Scandinavian gods. He rode about on a horse with eight legs and often disguised himself as an old man.

THURSDAY was "Thor's day." **Thor**, another son of Woden, was the Scandinavian thunder god. When he rode across the sky in his great chariot, the sound of the wheels made thunder.

FRIDAY honors Woden's wife **Frigga**. She had a lot of important jobs as goddess of love, beauty, marriage, childbearing, and the household, so she certainly deserved a day of her own. At first Friday was "Frigga's day."

SATURDAY, originally "Saturn's day," is named after **Saturn**, the Roman god of agriculture. In ancient times a rollicking seven-day harvest festival, Saturnalia, was held in his honor every year. Today many people like to have a jolly good time on Saturday night. So it's fitting that this day reminds us of Saturn.

If you're wondering about Sunday and Monday, they're not named after eponyms. Ancient people did name them after two bodies, though—heavenly bodies. Sunday was the "sun day" and Monday was the "moon day."

Months

Like most of the days of the week, five of the months are named after mythological gods and goddesses. Two other months honor real Roman leaders.

JANUARY is the month of **Janus**, the ancient Roman god of gates and doorways. He had two faces, so at the same time he could see the old year going and the new year coming. The word "janitor" comes from Janus. Originally, it meant just a doorkeeper; later it changed to the caretaker of the whole building.

MARCH comes from **Mars**, the Roman god of war.

APRIL is for Aphro, the nickname of **Aphrodite**, the Greek goddess of love and beauty.

MAY honors **Maia**, the Roman goddess of spring.

JUNE is for the goddess **Juno**, the patroness of marriage and the well-being of women.

JULY comes from **Julius Caesar's** first name. Caesar was an ancient Roman statesman and general who became a dictator. He was assassinated in 44 B.C.

AUGUST was named after Julius Caesar's adopted son, **Augustus Caesar**, the first Roman emperor.

The names of the other months did not come from eponyms. February was named after "februa," a Roman festival of purification held in the last month of the year in the Roman calendar. September, October, November, and December were named after the Latin words for seven, eight, nine, and ten because they were the seventh, eighth, ninth, and tenth months of the Roman year.

Measurements

Every day people need to measure things: the temperature, electricity, boundary lines, sound levels, even radioactivity. Many measuring words are eponymous. Weigh these.

Temperature—Fahrenheit and Celsius

The two main scales for measuring temperature, Fahrenheit and Celsius, are named for two eighteenth-century scientists.

The Fahrenheit scale, on which water freezes at 32° and boils at 212°, was devised by **Gabriel Fahrenheit**, a German physicist.

On the Celsius scale (the official name of the centigrade scale), the freezing point of water is 0° and the boiling point is 100°. A Swedish astronomer, **Anders Celsius**, established this scale.

Electricity — Volt, Ohm, Ampere, and Watt

When you study electricity in science, you learn about "volts," "ohms," "amperes," and "watts." These are common terms used to measure electrical force, electrical resistance, current strength, and electrical power. Look up one of these terms in the dictionary and you'll find the other terms in the definition. All four words come from eponyms. They honor the following scientists:

Alessandro Volta, 1745–1827, an Italian physicist;

Georg Ohm, 1787–1854, a German physicist;

André-Marie Ampère, 1775–1836, a French physicist; and

James Watt, 1736–1819, a Scottish engineer and inventor.

Mason-Dixon Line

Pennsylvania and Maryland were having a dispute in the 1760s. Exactly where did one state end and the other begin? Two English surveyors, **Charles Mason** and **Jeremiah Dixon**, spent four years figuring out a boundary line. On maps the Mason-Dixon Line separated the free Northern states and the slave-owning Southern states during the Civil War. Today some people still call it the dividing line between the northern and southern states.

Decibel

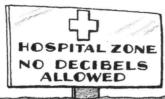

The loudness of a sound is measured in "decibels." One decibel is the lowest sound that the human ear can hear. Ten decibels make one "bel." "Bel" is named for **Alexander Graham Bell**, a Scot who came to America in 1870. Besides inventing the telephone, Bell developed many electronic devices for people who are deaf.

Geiger Counter

Hans Geiger, a German physicist who died in 1945, invented this clicking instrument, which detects and measures radioactivity and cosmic rays.

∘ 7 ∘

Bad Guy, Good Guy

Here are five bad guys (hooligan, hoodlum, thug, vandal, and scrooge), one good guy (bobby), and one guy who's his own guy (maverick). But first, the word "guy" itself.

Guy

Guy Fawkes tried to blow up Parliament and King James I of England on November 5, 1605, but he was caught before the gunpowder exploded. Ever since, November 5 has been Guy Fawkes Day in England. Children make dummies of Guy out of rags and call them "guys." In England a "guy" is a weird-looking man, but in America "guy" is just slang for any fellow.

Hooligan

In the 1890s there was a popular song in England about a rough guy named **Patrick Hooligan**. The songwriter claimed that a real street rowdy by that name had once actually led a violent gang of brawling, thieving boys who caused a lot of trouble. Today "hooligan" refers to any petty crook or young ruffian.

Hoodlum

A dangerous gangster named **Muldoon** terrorized San Francisco in the 1870s, according to one tale. A reporter wrote a story about him but was afraid to tell his real name, so he spelled it backwards—"Noodlum." The printer thought the *N* was an *H* and typed the name "Hoodlum." Soon all small-time crooks were called "hoodlums" or "hoods."

Thug

For hundreds of years, a gang of well-organized professional tough guys roamed northern India, brutally robbing and slaughtering people. They were called **Thugs** (from the Indian word "thag," which means a cheat or thief.) Now we call any cutthroat hoodlum or violent hooligan a "thug."

Vandal

In A.D. 455, eighty thousand wild members of a fierce Germanic tribe called the **Vandals** stormed into Rome, Italy, robbing the people and setting fire to the beautiful buildings. Before they got to Italy, the Vandals had been just as bad in France, Spain, and northern Africa. Today anyone who maliciously destroys public or private property is called a "vandal."

Scrooge

A "scrooge" is a mean miser because **Ebenezer Scrooge**, the grumpy villain-hero of Charles Dickens's world-famous book *A Christmas Carol* (published in 1843) is a mean miser. (At the end of the story, you may remember, Scrooge becomes a nice guy.)

Bobby

In England a police officer is affectionately called a "bobby." This slang word comes from the nickname of **Sir Robert "Bobby" Peel**, a famous statesman who reorganized the London police force in 1829.

Maverick

Someone owed Texan **Samuel Maverick** a debt in the mid-1800s and paid with cattle. Maverick didn't brand them all with the name of his ranch. Soon unbranded cattle who didn't stay with their herd were called "Maverick's." Now the word "maverick" means a nonconformist, a person who keeps apart from the crowd and does his or her own thing.

°8°

Epo-Things

Many things—workaday and exotic, historical and musical, gigantic and hand-held, cuddly and deadly—were named after people, usually their inventors. However, one of the men mentioned below was very upset that he became an eponym.

Listerine®

An eminent British doctor **Joseph Lister**, the father of antiseptic surgery, was famous in the 1800s for perfecting methods of killing germs that caused infection. In 1881, when an American company introduced a mouthwash that claimed to kill germs, it named the product after Dr. Lister.

Run for your life!

Ferris Wheel

People running the 1893 Chicago World's Fair wanted a spectacular attraction. So **George Washington Ferris**, an inventor and engineer from Illinois, designed a huge, upright, revolving wheel. Ferris's wheel carried almost 1500 riders up and around and was a tremendous success. You can ride a Ferris wheel today at most fairs and amusement parks.

Jacuzzi®

In 1958, seven Jacuzzi brothers invented a whirlpool pump for one of their sons who had been born with arthritis. The pump sent jets of warm water swirling all around the sick boy in the bathtub and made him feel better. In 1968, **Roy Jacuzzi**, the grandson of one of the brothers, expanded the idea by inventing a whirlpool bath and later a whirlpool spa.

Bunsen Burner

Professor **Robert Bunsen**, a German chemist, needed a hot, smokeless flame for his scientific experiments. Earlier devices weren't good enough, so in 1855 Dr. Bunsen developed his own. It was a small metal tube on a stand that burned a mixture of gas and air. Today you'll find Dr. Bunsen's burner in many school and scientific laboratories.

Guillotine

Joseph Guillotin was a kindly doctor during the French Revolution. He made a famous speech urging that France use a beheading machine for fast, merciful executions. When people called the contraption a "guillotine," the doctor was distressed. After he died, his children urged the government to change the name of this death device. The government said no, so the children changed their own names!

Derrick

A derrick is a large, motorized crane used for lifting heavy objects on oil rigs and construction sites. **Godfrey Derrick**, a famous London hangman in the early 1600s, redesigned the original gallows into something like a crane. People called Derrick's improved gallows the "derrick." Later "derrick" came to mean any lifting device.

Teddy Bear

Theodore "Teddy" Roosevelt, the twenty-sixth president of the United States (1901-1909), loved to hunt. His hosts on a Mississippi hunting trip tied a small bear to a tree so that the president would have something to shoot, but Roosevelt let the bear go. A newspaper published a famous drawing of the scene. Starting in 1902, manufacturers of stuffed toy bears began calling them "teddy bears" in honor of the president.

Frisbee®

About fifty years ago drivers from the **Frisbie Pie Company** in Connecticut used to throw around tin pie plates—marked "Frisbie"—to amuse themselves on their lunch breaks. The activity caught on at Yale University nearby, and then at other colleges. In the 1950s a California factory began manufacturing a plastic throwing disk and called it "Frisbee" in honor of the Frisbie Pie Company.

Guppy

R. J. Lechmere Guppy, president of the Scientific Association of Trinidad, discovered little tropical fish on that South American island. In 1868 he brought specimens to the British Museum, which put them on display. Today guppies are popular aquarium fish in many homes. The males are very colorful, and the females can have up to 185 babies at one time!

Saxophone and Sousaphone

If you ever saw a jazz band on television or watched a marching band in a parade, you saw these two musical instruments.

The saxophone, a wind instrument popular with jazz musicians, was first played in Paris in 1844 by its inventor, Belgian instrument maker **Antoine Joseph Sax**. Sax lost his way in the music when demonstrating his new instrument, and he held one note until he found his place. The French audience loved the long sound! Today musicians often hold one note when playing the saxophone.

Half a century later **John Philip Sousa** devised his sousaphone for marching bands. It's a large, circular tuba with a full, rich sound. Sousa, America's most famous bandmaster, composed over one hundred popular marches and was known as the "March King." At first he conducted the U.S. Marine band, but later he toured the world with his own band.

Pompadour

The Marquise de Pompadour, the beautiful, intelligent mistress and advisor of King Louis XV of France, set the style for fashions in the 1700s. She wore her hair puffed straight up from her forehead, and although many things (a dress, a bird, colors, etc.) have been called "pompadour" after her, she is best known for her elaborate hairdo.

Sideburns

General Ambrose Burnside thought up bizarre schemes to win the Civil War and almost got thrown out of the Union army. Later he was elected governor and senator from Rhode Island. He was a fancy dresser whose picture often appeared in the papers. Men copied the original way Burnside wore big whiskers down the sides of his face. They called the hair "burnsides," then switched it to "sideburns."

Braille

Louis Braille, a three-year-old French boy, had an accident that left him blind. Later he became a student, and then a teacher, at a school for the blind in Paris. In 1829 he published a system for printing books with raised dots that stood for letters, numbers, and punctuation. Today people who are blind can read books in braille by feeling the dots with their fingers.

Morse Code

In Morse code long and short beeps, or flashes of light, represent letters, numbers, and punctuation. People can communicate with each other over long distances with these "dots and dashes." **Samuel F. B. Morse**, a painter and inventor, devised this system to send messages over America's first telegraph line between Washington and Baltimore in 1843. Morse code is used all over the world today. The international distress signal SOS (···−−−···) is one of the best-known code patterns.

Rugby

In England people play a form of football called "rugby." Players on the two opposing teams may kick, dribble, or run with the oval ball. But they can't throw a forward pass, substitute players, or call a time-out. Rugby was invented at **Rugby**, a school for boys, in **Rugby**, a town in central England. So naturally the game is called "rugby."

Marathon

In 490 B.C. the Greeks won a famous battle at **Marathon**, a plain in eastern Greece. A messenger ran twenty-six miles to bring the good news from Marathon to Athens. Today a race of twenty-six miles or any contest that requires great endurance or time is called a "marathon."

The Most Famous
Eponymous Word
in the World

What do you think is the most famous word that came from an eponym? It isn't even really a word. It's more of an expression, but everybody knows it. People all over the world use it.

Where did it come from? From the name of a place and the nickname of a president.

Kinderhook is a little country town in upstate New York. It was on a farm there that Martin Van Buren was born in 1782. Even as a boy Martin loved politics, and when he grew up he became a state legislator, U.S. senator, governor of New York, secretary of state, and vice-president of the United States. But he wanted to go even higher, and he was elected the eighth president of the United States in 1836.

He ran for reelection in 1840. It was a tough campaign. More voters in America at that time came from small towns than from big cities, and Van Buren wanted to show that he had come from a small town too. So he started calling himself **"Old Kinderhook"** after his hometown. He even set up "Old Kinderhook" political clubs. "Old Kinderhook" soon got shortened to just "OK," and signs were painted that read: "Vote Right. Vote OK." "OK" soon came to mean "All right. All correct. Just fine. Terrific."

Martin Van Buren lost the election and became a rather forgotten president in our history books. But his nickname has lived on as one of the most popular expressions in the world. **OK**?

Alphabetical list of the
words featured in this book.

Other Books About Eponyms

If you want to learn more about eponyms, you might like to read some of the following books that the author used in his research.

Boycott, Rosie, **Batty, Bloomers and Boycott**, New York: Peter Bedrick Books, 1983.

Perl, Lila, **Blue Monday and Friday the Thirteenth**, New York: Clarion Books, 1986.

Hendrickson, Robert, **The Dictionary of Eponyms**, (published in hardcover as **Human Words**). New York: Stein and Day, 1985.

Pizer, Vernon, **Take My Word for It**, New York: Dodd, Mead & Company, 1981.

Word Mysteries and Histories, The Editors of The American Heritage Dictionaries, Boston: Houghton Mifflin Company, 1986.

Smith, Don and Peter Porges, **Words Alive!**, New York: Scholastic Book Services, 1979.

———. **Words Alive Again!** New York: Scholastic Book Services, 1980.

Other Clarion Word Play Books

Easy as Pie
A Guessing Game of Sayings
By Marcia and Michael Folsom
Illustrated in three colors by Jack Kent

Eight Ate
A Feast of Homonym Riddles
By Marvin Terban
Illustrated in two colors by Giulio Maestro

In a Pickle
And Other Funny Idioms
By Marvin Terban
Illustrated in two colors by Giulio Maestro

I Think I Thought
And Other Tricky Verbs
By Marvin Terban
Illustrated in two colors by Giulio Maestro

Mad as a Wet Hen!
And Other Funny Idioms
By Marvin Terban
Illustrated in two colors by Giulio Maestro

Q is for Duck

An Alphabet Guessing Game
By Mary Elting and Michael Folsom
Illustrated in three colors by Jack Kent

Razzle-Dazzle Riddles

Written and illustrated in two colors by Giulio Maestro

Riddle Romp

Written and illustrated in two colors by Giulio Maestro

Too Hot to Hoot

Funny Palindrome Riddles
By Marvin Terban
Illustrated in two colors by Giulio Maestro

What's a Frank Frank?

Tasty Homograph Riddles
Written and illustrated in two colors by Giulio Maestro

What's Mite Might?

Homophone Riddles to Boost Your Word Power
Written and illustrated in two colors by Giulio Maestro

Your Foot's on My Feet!

And Other Tricky Nouns
By Marvin Terban
Illustrated in two colors by Giulio Maestro

About the Author

Marvin Terban has been teaching fifth and sixth grade English at Columbia Grammar and Preparatory School in Manhattan for almost twenty-five years. Many of his word play books began as grammar games in his classroom where he delights his students by finding new ways to teach language skills. He also directs children's plays during the summer at Cejwin Camps, Port Jervis, New York. In addition to teaching and writing, Mr. Terban is an actor and has appeared in many community theater productions and several films. He lives in Manhattan with his wife, Karen, and their two children, David, 16, and Jennifer, 11, and a menagerie of pets.

About the Artist

Giulio Maestro grew up in New York City and graduated from The Cooper Union Art School. For several years, he was a designer for an advertising/promotion firm before he began working on children's books. Of the over 100 books he has illustrated, 30 are by his author/wife, Betsy Maestro. Mr. Maestro has written and illustrated four Clarion riddle books of his own: **Riddle Romp**, **What's a Frank Frank?**, **What's Mite Might?**, and **Razzle-Dazzle Riddles**. The Maestros have two children, Daniela, 12, and Marco, 9. Their home and studio is a renovated barn in Old Lyme, Connecticut.